St Edmundsbury Cathedral

FRONT COVER: *The south side of the cathedral, showing the new east end, completed in 1970.*

ABOVE: *The west front showing the new porch. Notice the shells of St James in the stonework.*

BACK COVER: *An aerial view of the cathedral, showing clearly the old north side.*

St Edmundsbury Cathedral

The Mother Church of Suffolk

*"Lord, I have loved the habitation of thy house
and the place where thine honour dwelleth."*

The parish church of St James, Bury St Edmunds, became a cathedral as recently as August 1913 when the diocese of St Edmundsbury and Ipswich was created. But its story, linked as it is with that of the Benedictine Abbey of St Edmundsbury, one of the greatest shrines in Christendom, goes back to A.D. 870 when Edmund, the young Christian Saxon king of East Anglia, surrendered his life to the invading Danes to avoid his country being completely despoiled. He was tied to a tree at Hoxne, according to one tradition, and his body pierced through with arrows and beheaded. The legend, which grew up after his death, tells how his friends were guided to the body of their beloved king by the cries of a wolf which was guarding it, an incident enshrined in the Borough arms whose motto is: "Shrine of the King, Cradle of the Law".

It was to the Saxon town of Beodricsworth, which soon after became known as St Edmundsbury, that they brought the body of their martyred king about A.D. 903 and there it was guarded by a small body of clerics in a wooden church of large dimensions. In 1010 there was an invasion by Danish pirates who landed at Ipswich, and in alarm the body was transferred to London where it remained for three years before being returned to St Edmundsbury. In 1020 the secular clergy were turned out by Aelfwin, Bishop of Elmham, and Benedictine monks took their place as the guardians of the shrine of the king to which pilgrims were now coming from far and wide. Under the first abbot, Uvius, the monks replaced the wooden church by a new stone Abbey dedicated in 1032 with the help of King Canute who gave his crown towards the cost. The third Abbey Church, the extensive remains of which are still to be seen and of which the Norman Tower was the entrance gate, was built by Abbot Baldwin (1065–97) and his successors. This magnificent Norman edifice, which with its adjoining monastic buildings must have resembled Ely Cathedral, became one of the greatest and wealthiest centres of Christianity in the land, a leading place of pilgrimage, and a famous seat of learning and scholarship.

★

LEFT: *The new porch from the east, showing the building of the first eight bays of the cloisters which were dedicated during 1961. Some have been erectd as memorials. In the future it is hoped to continue the cloisters to the vestries and other parts of the extension yet to be built.*

FACING PAGE: *The west end from the south aisle.*

Among the abbots who served it were Anselm, nephew of the Saint (1121–48), and Samson (1182–1211), made famous by Carlyle.

One event which happened in the Abbey of St Edmundsbury gives to Bury St Edmunds, as the town came to be called in the 15th century, the claim to be regarded as the Cradle of the Law, birthplace of the principles of justice upon which the freedom and democracy of our western civilisation is built. On St Edmund's Day, 20th November 1214, the barons swore at the High Altar that they would compel King John to seal a Charter of Liberty, which later he did at Runnymede. This event was commemorated in the town in 1959 by a colourful Magna Carta Pageant. 1970 was proclaimed "St Edmunds Year" and there were great celebrations of the 1100th anniversary of St Edmund's martyrdom, including a pageant play "Edmund of Anglia".

The story of the great Abbey is full of vicissitudes. There were times of crisis in the local risings of 1327 and 1381. Both the central and western towers fell down, the former in 1210, the latter in 1430. The first was rebuilt, the other may not ever have been completely restored. A great fire in 1465 gutted the interior of the building. When the monastery was dissolved in 1539, the commissioners did great damage to the Abbey, sold the bells and confiscated much of the plate and other property. The townspeople completed the work of destruction. The shrine of St Edmund was stripped and broken. The present location of the Saint's body is unknown, and although there is a widely accepted theory that it was removed, there is every possibility that the despoilers may have had some reverence for the royal bones.

The Abbey would have been spared if the attempts of Bishop Herfast and his successor, Herbert de Losinga, to establish their see in Bury St Edmunds instead of Norwich had been successful and it had become a cathedral in the 11th century. Centuries later Henry VIII had the idea of creating a new see with the Abbey as its cathedral. This too, would have prevented the Abbey's destruction. But it came to naught. It might also have been spared if there had been need of the building as a parish church at the time of the Dissolution. But the monks had provided in the monastery three magnificent churches for the people, St Mary and St James, which still function side by side, and St Margaret's, of which only a few traces remain. Here we are

ABOVE: *Sir Gilbert Scott's ceiling completed in the Victorian restoration programme and decorated in traditional East Anglian style in 1982.*

RIGHT: *The main hammer beams terminate with angels and shields bearing alternately the scallop-shell, the wallet and the staff of St James, the crown and arrows of St Edmund, and the Cross of St George.*

FACING PAGE: *The majestic nave is nearly 140 feet long and 70 feet wide. The total length of quire and nave is 248 feet. It was re-roofed by Sir Gilbert Scott in the last century. The great arch and everything beyond is part of the extension begun in 1959 and completed in 1970. The 1000 kneelers have been embroidered by women of the diocese.*

concerned chiefly with the story of St James' church which became the cathedral of the new diocese of St Edmundsbury and Ipswich in 1914, although the beautiful parish church of St Mary has a great history of its own and is full of treasures. The present cathedral church is the second church of St James to be built on the site. The first was built by Abbot Anselm who was prevented from going on a pilgrimage to the traditional site of the grave of St James at Compostello in Spain. Nothing is left of the church which preceded the present cathedral except the stone shafts which were built into the outer side of the north wall of the present building and which are still clearly to be seen.

The nave of the cathedral, as we now see it, was largely built, we believe, by John Wastell, one of the greatest of the 15th-century church builders who lived most of his life in Bury St Edmunds where he died in 1515. He also built part of the Chapel of King's College, Cambridge, the Bell Harry Tower of Canterbury Cathedral and parish churches such as that at Saffron Walden.

The cathedral has a fine west front with rich medieval moulding and panelling with the emblems of St James (the staff and wallet and scallop shell) and of St John (the chalice surmounted by the dragon). It is interesting to compare the 15th-century craftsmanship with the work on the new north-west porch completed and dedicated by Dr Fisher, then Archbishop of Canterbury, on 19th July, 1960. The new work, of which Mr Stephen Dykes Bower is the architect and which has been done by the local masons, compares very favourably with the old. It was the first part, costing £25,000, of the Cathedral Extension Scheme, fuller details of which are given later. On either side of the new entrance to the nave are carved the arms of the Province of Canterbury and of the diocese of St Edmundsbury and Ipswich.

The Cloisters

The first eight bays of the cloisters were also built in 1960. The first is to the memory of the late Provost White whose patient work laid the foundations of the Extension plans; the second bay has been provided by the Freemasons of Suffolk as a memorial to the late Earl of Stradbroke, and another is a memorial to Bishop Hodgson, the first bishop of the diocese. The cloisters, which are glazed, are used in the summer months for exhibitions of Christian art and literature and for missionary displays. Ultimately they will lead to the new vestries, meeting rooms, offices and the Chapter House, all yet to be built.

Entering the cathedral by the new porch, one's eye is caught by the splendour of the font and its canopy, 20 feet 3 inches in height, the work of Mr F. E. Howard, an Oxford craftsman. It was provided as a memorial to those of the cathedral parish who gave their lives in the First World War, many of whom were christened at this font. But the decoration in the medieval manner was done as recently as 1960 by the Friends of the Cathedral when the font was moved to its present position at the west end of the central aisle. Over the new door is placed the golden cherub blowing a trumpet. This had originally been a part of the first organ case which was removed from the west end. The cherub was discovered in an antique shop in

*

LEFT: *The Lady Chapel was completed in 1970. The Mother's Union of the diocese contributed generously to its cost and provided, with other bodies, its furnishings.*

FACING PAGE: *A superb view of the High Altar looking through the quire to the great west window. Lined oak stalls are provided for 24 Honorary Canons who with the Provost, Canons Residentiary and Diocesan staff form the Cathedral Chapter. Stalls are also provided for eight Lay Canons. It is here that the cathedral choir of 24 trebles drawn from local schools, and 14 men offer worship to Almighty God.*

Belgium and restored to the cathedral. Below the cherub are the royal arms of King Charles II dated about 1670.

Looking eastward from the font the visitor is impressed by the magnificence of the nave which is 135 feet 10 inches in length and 71 feet 9 inches wide at the west end. It is divided into nine bays by lofty and slender pillars. It was started about 1502, the west end being commenced first. The work progressed slowly and was still unfinished when the architect, John Wastell, died in 1515 at the age of 55. After the Reformation, King Edward VI gave £200 to assist completion of the work.

The original roof surmounting the nave was of richly ornamented panelled timber of very low pitch. It was removed in 1777 and replaced by a new one of deal with a false ceiling of stucco. The present roof is a part of the Victorian restoration of the building which the eminent architect, Sir Gilbert Scott, undertook in the 1860's, a restoration which has features typical of the period and which some people tend to regret. This high-pitched oak roof, of hammer-beam construction, was introduced by the people of St James' to emulate the much finer roof of their neighbour, St Mary's. The principals are terminated by angels holding shields ensigned alternately with the scallop shell, the wallet and staff of St James, the crown and arrows of St Edmund, and the Cross of St George. The colour which enlivens the nave roof was applied 1948–49 when the nave was cleaned and restored by the Friends of the Cathedral. The decoration of the roof was completed in 1982 and funded by an anonymous donor. The roofs of the aisles are 16th century.

★

LEFT: *The Susanna Window. This is the most valuable glass in the cathedral and one of its greatest treasures. It is the westernmost window of the south aisle. This window, which is more fully described on page 10, consists of medieval glass collected from various parts of the church and arranged in 1828. The upper lights portray saints and kings. The lower three lights tell the story of Susanna and the Elders, and are of 15th-century Flemish glass of the Brussels school.*

FACING PAGE: *This view of the nave from the south aisle gives an impression of the rich 19th-century glass which fills the nave windows.*

The Nave Windows

Only one of the magnificent stained-glass windows is old, namely the last window on the south-west side of the aisle. It is filled with original glass, collected from various parts of the building in 1828, some of it believed to be 14th-century. It is generally called the Susanna Window because the three lower lights represent the story from the Apocrypha of Susanna and the Elders. This is 15th-century Flemish glass. The upper lights show parts of a Jesse tree, some kings and a bishop, St Joachim, father of the Virgin Mary carrying a lamb, two figures, perhaps Cain and Abel, St Catherine and kneeling angels with green wings. This window is of a period little represented in England, the best example being the windows of King's College, Cambridge. The rest of the nave windows, 20 altogether, are completely filled with fairly modern glass and are regarded as the best collection of their period. The windows in the north all depict Old Testament scenes, and those in the south portray New Testament scenes. The great west window, showing the Last Judgment, is particularly fine and may be seen to best effect from the step of the chancel.

The Chandeliers

The cathedral is particularly fortunate in having a complete set of light fittings, designed by Stephen Dykes Bower and made by Eric Stevenson, a Gold Medalist blacksmith from Wroxham, Norfolk. Of modern design, with gold plated fittings, they fit in well with the new and old parts of the building, without in any way being obtrusive.

The Quire

This replaces the three chancels which have gone before since the church was built. The third, a part of the restoration by Sir Gilbert Scott in the last century, was demolished in 1963. Its former east window, by Hardman, representing the Transfiguration with scenes in the life of St James, is at present in storage together with the oak roof. The present three east windows by Kempe, representing the Nativity, Crucifixion and Ascension, were formerly on the north and south sides of the previous chancel. A small amount of extra glass was added to fit them into their present position where their great beauty is better seen than ever before. They are fully comparable with medieval glass.

The unusual altar cross and candlesticks on the High Altar are of modern craftsmanship. They were given by Mrs John Greene, in memory of an only child. The High Altar rails were given in memory of Bishop Richard Brook, a former bishop of the diocese who died in 1969.

In 1984 to commemorate the 70th anniversary of the Cathedral and Diocese, the Friends of the Cathedral commissioned the embellishment of the High Altar. The "Sun Burst" was designed in wrought iron and semi precious stones by Stephen Dykes Bower and the work was carried out by E. Furneaux of Great Dunmow.

Note the beautiful painting of the roof of the quire.

The Bishop's Throne

The quire also contains the Bishop's Throne, a superb piece of modern craftsmanship from the same hand as the font cover. Standing 25 feet high, it possesses fine canopies and delicate pinnacles, with a boss in the vaulting of the crown and arrows of St Edmund. The winged buttresses are surmounted by wolves guarding the head of St Edmund. The throne is a memorial to Dr Hodgson, the first bishop, who is buried in the Sanctuary.

The Choir and Canons' stalls were made by local craftsmen in 1970 and form the memorial of Mr F. W. Choat. Each of the stalls occupied by an Honorary Canon bears a name outstanding in the history of the Church in East Anglia or of the Abbey. Recently some extra stalls were given the name of a famous modern churchman, and in accordance with the ecumenical spirit of the age one was named after Pope John

Continued on page 14

★

LEFT (above): *St Edmund's Cross with its crown and arrows was presented by the Readers in 1964, the Jubilee Year, when it was carried in procession into every parish. It was designed by Mr Jack Penton, of Suffolk, and made by Mr H. B. Moore, a Suffolk craftsman.*

LEFT (below): *The Bishop's Throne is described in detail on this page. This carving of the traditional incident of the wolf guarding King Edmund's head is a prominent feature. The throne is a memorial to Bishop H. B. Hodgson, the first bishop of the diocese whose remains are buried in the Sanctuary close by.*

FACING PAGE: *The south transept contains a new memorial tablet to commemorate the Ven. H. R. Norton in whose memory the Sanctus Bell has been placed in the south turret.*

ABOVE: *The west end of the nave. The magnificent west window by Hardman depicts the Last Judgement. The font canopy was provided as a 1914–18 war memorial and was decorated with colour in 1960.*
FACING PAGE: *The quire. The roof of the new quire is gaily coloured. The nave altar under the crossing has altar rails on three sides. Light fittings made by Mr. E. Stevenson won the gold medal of the Blacksmiths' Company.*

XXIII. The cushions in the stalls embroidered voluntarily by local people are worth examination.

The Organ

The Grand Organ ranks among the finest instruments in the country and contains 6,650 pipes. Of four manuals, 79 pistons and 96 stops, it incorporates some of the pipes which were in the Walker organ of 1860, and it also retains some solo stops from the Norman and Beard organ of 1914. The organ as it now stands (still awaiting its case when funds permit) is the work of the Worcestershire firm of Nicholson, and came into use in 1970.

The pedal section includes a splendid reed section with a mighty 32 foot Contra Ophicleide and a brilliant four rank Mixture. The solo section is notable for its thrilling Trompeta Real ('royal trumpet') which comes into its own on the cathedral's big ceremonial occasions.

A fully descriptive leaflet on the organ may be purchased at the bookstall.

The Lady Chapel Organ

This delightful little chamber organ was built in 1790 by Henry Holland of Bath and London and was brought from London by wagon in the year of Waterloo, 1815, to Walsingham Abbey, Norfolk. It was found in St Margaret's Church, Hales, Norfolk and on the closure of that church in 1968 it was presented to the cathedral. It has been restored and is frequently in use.

The St Edmund Chapel Organ

This interesting organ was built by Thomas Casson around 1905 for use in the Crypt Chapel of St Paul's Cathedral, London. It was eventually replaced by a

★

LEFT (above): *The interior of the north-west porch.*

LEFT (below): *The St Edmund's Chapel provides a subdued atmosphere for meditation and private prayer. Here the Blessed Sacrament is reserved. Both the stained-glass window and the reredos are from the old east end, rebuilt in 1970. The brass candlestick was a gift from the Roman Catholic Diocese of Bruges to mark the 70th Anniversary of the Diocese of St Edmundsbury and Ipswich in 1984.*

FACING PAGE: *The entrance to St Edmunds Chapel through magnificent wrought iron gates given by the Friends of the Cathedral.*

larger organ and lost sight of. It was discovered in 1973 in a derelict and unplayable condition in a school chapel in the south of England and was purchased and restored by a group of well wishers and presented to the cathedral. The casework is of interest and the instrument is powerful enough to lead the singing of quite a large congregation.

The Chapels

The new Lady Chapel on the south side and St Edmund's Chapel on the north side contain furnishings by local craftsmen. Most of the furnishings in the Lady Chapel have been given by women of Suffolk. Notice the magnificent wrought iron gates to both chapels given by the Friends of the Cathedral. In St Edmund's Chapel there is on display a tapestry on the life of St Edmund made by the children of the schools of West Suffolk as their contribution to St Edmund Year, 1970, the 1100th anniversary of the martyrdom. The brick wall on which it hangs will be removed if ever the plan for further extension is made possible.

The Crossing

The crossing containing the nave altar was built between 1967–70 at a cost of over £220,000, as a memorial to Mrs Florence Maclean Vestey by her husband, Mr Ronald Vestey of Thurlow Hall, the cathedral's greatest benefactor in recent years. The south transept contains a number of memorial tablets to Bury families and a new one to commemorate the late Archdeacon Hugh Norton in whose memory the Sanctus Bell in the south turret has been installed. It was previously in the tower of the parish church at Stanton and is dated 1620.

Memorials

The chief sculpture in St James' is a monument by the west door depicting James Reynolds, Chief Baron of the Court of the Exchequer, sitting in judge's robes with cherubs drawing back the curtains, one holding a torch and one weeping, with a third set aloft and blowing a trumpet. In the cloisters are two marble portraits, a Chantrey medallion of the Rev E. V. Blomfield and a marble of Benjamin Malkin, once headmaster of King Edward VI School. This part of the cathedral contains a number of memorials to former masters and scholars of the school. The lectern and the bible upon it commemorate Bishop W. G. Whittingham, Lord Bishop of the Diocese between 1923–40.

The Bell Tower

This is regarded by many as one of the finest Norman buildings in the land. It was built for Abbot Anselm who called it the Tower of St James. It is 86 feet high and 36 feet square with walls nearly six feet thick. It contains a fine peal of ten bells which were made in 1785 by the recasting of the six old bells. The great arch once had a sculpture of Christ in Glory in its head, but it was removed in 1789 to afford freer passage for loads of hay and straw. The original ground level was as it now is at the base of the tower.

Present and Future Plans

The consecration of the quire and crossing on 29th September 1970, brought to an end the main phase in the great work of cathedral extension which was envisaged in 1914 but prevented from being achieved by the two wars, and the economic depressions that have filled most of this century. The building, which began in 1959, has cost over £600,000 which has been raised during

Continued on page 18

THIS PAGE: *The Abbey ruins are in the custody of the Ministry of Works which is conducting extensive excavations. The most substantial parts of the Abbey Church still remaining are the buried crypt, the columns of the central tower, a portion of the north transept, seen in the picture, left, and most of the impressive west front, illustrated above. An attractive feature is the houses which have been built into the arches. The statue of St Edmund, martyred boy King of East Anglia is the work of Elizabeth Frink. It was commissioned to mark the amalgamation of the two counties of East and West Suffolk in local government re-organisation in 1972. It stands off-centre from the processional route down Churchgate Street, through the Norman Tower to the great west doors set into the central arches of the old Abbey.*

FACING PAGE: *The Norman Tower is regarded as one of the finest Norman buildings in the country. It was the grand portal of the Abbey of St Edmund, facing its great west door. It still serves as the bell tower of St James' Cathedral.*

Edmunds. There is the 13th-century Abbot's Bridge, there is Moyses Hall, in the market place, once a Norman dwelling house and now a museum, and above all there is the noble church of St Mary, the burial place of Mary Tudor, sister of Henry VIII, with its superb angel roof. Truly Bury St Edmunds is a treasure that has few equals in a land full of treasures.

The Site of the Abbey of Saint Edmund

"A man who saw the abbey would say verily it were a city; so many gates there are in it, and some of brass; so many towers and a most stately church, upon which attend three other churches also standing gloriously in the same churchyard, all of passing fine and curious workmanship." (John Leland, c. 1534).

In the year 869 Edmund, King of East Angles, was martyred by the heathen Danish invaders. His remains were brought to Bury St Edmunds and pilgrims resorted to this place to do honour to his memory. His fame spread widely and for long he could truly be called the national saint of England. In 1020 a body of Benedictine monks became custodians of the shrine. This was the beginning of the Abbey of St Edmund.

★

a period of inflation and rising costs.

Lots of things remain unfinished; the tower, for example, is not there, nor is the rest of the cloister and the north transept, all of which have been started. Some essential furnishings are missing, notably an organ case, but a start has been made on this in memory of Harley Drayton. Much work has not even been started, chiefly the vestries, offices and meeting rooms. But a glorious building has been created of which Suffolk should be proud. The cathedral is much better equipped to do its job, but a great many people who are not perhaps much concerned about that aspect are becoming filled with admiration that local craftsmen have in these days been able to create a building as beautiful as a medieval church. It is surely the most splendid East Anglian building of this century, and one that will bear witness to the skill of the builders and the vision of those who have worked to achieve it for many centuries to come. One day we hope that benefactors will enable us or our successors to finish the work completely.

As well as its cathedral, its Norman and medieval gateways, and its fascinating Abbey ruins set in the midst of the lovely Abbey Gardens, the town has many other architectural gems to delight its visitors. There are, in fact, buildings of almost every period of English architecture in its fine old streets and squares. The Angel Hill is as good an example of this as any place in England with its Dickensian inn, its Georgian houses, its 14th-century Abbey Gate, and its Athenaeum Ballroom. But Angel Hill does not exhaust the treasures of Bury St

LEFT (above): *The Abbot's Bridge. Another of the few remains of the Abbey buildings still surviving is the Abbot's Bridge, an ancient bridge three arches across the River Lark, which carried a curtain wall across the stream.*

LEFT (below): *The Magna Carta Pillar. On one of the pillars that sustained the central tower of the Abbey Church visitors will see a tablet which commemorates the fact that on St Edmund's Day, 20th November, 1214, the barons swore at St Edmund's altar to obtain from King John a charter of liberties later ratified at Runnymede.*

FACING PAGE: *The Abbey Gate. This noble 14th-century gate which leads from Angel Hill into the Abbey Gardens was the entrance to the great court of the Abbot's Palace. It is 50 feet long, 41 feet broad, and 62 feet high. The front is of rich Gothic design with a doorway 18 feet wide. The canopied niches originally contained the figures of saints.*

from medieval times. The Chapel of the Charnel was built in *c.* 1300 by Abbot John of Northwold, with a crypt below to contain the bones cast up from previous burials.

The west front is the largest surviving portion of the great Abbey Church. With the dwelling houses which have been built into it since the dissolution of the monastery in 1539, this has now rather the appearance of a "folly".

The Norman Tower was built by Abbot Anselm (1121–48) as an entrance gate to both the Abbey Church and the churchyard. It later became the bell tower of St James Church, now the cathedral.

The Story of the Tapestry

The conception of this work came to Olga Ironside Wood when she wrote and presented, by invitation of the Borough of Bury St Edmunds, her outdoor play "Edmund of Anglia", with a cast of hundreds, in the Abbey Gardens during July 1970, to commemorate the 1100th anniversary of the Saint's death by martyrdom.

She discovered that very few school children, and even fewer adults, knew the story of King Edmund's life, and the idea of a "bayeux" gradually took shape.

A talented young teacher from Brandon, David Orchard, who designed and

★

The Abbey Gate, entrance to the great courtyard of the monastery, was built following the rising of the townspeople in 1327, when the previous gateway was destroyed. The gate (a fine example of the Decorated period) was therefore built as much for defence as for ornament; on the west side arrow slits may be seen behind the niches formerly containing the figures of saints. Another notable feature is the great east window which foreshadows the Perpendicular style of the following century.

The Abbot's Bridge was built shortly after the Abbey had acquired in *c.* 1211 a vineyard on the far side of the River Lark. The bridge stands against the earlier wall of the precinct: holes on the north side of this wall show where poles supported a plank bridge for the use of the townspeople.

The Chapter House was the scene of the discovery in 1906 of the remains of five of the abbots of St Edmund. Among these was the famous Abbot Samson (1182–1211), hero of the contemporary *Chronicle* of Jocelyn of Brakelond.

According to the chronicle of Roger of Wendover the site of the High Altar of the Abbey Church was the meeting place in November, 1214, of a number of the barons of England, who here took oath that they would compel King John to grant them their lawful rights, if need be by force of arms. The sealing of *Magna Carta* by the king at Runnymede on 15th June, 1215, provided the sequel. A considerable area close to the high altar site is now being excavated to the original floor level by the Department of the Environment.

The churchyard occupying the south side of the precinct was a place of burial

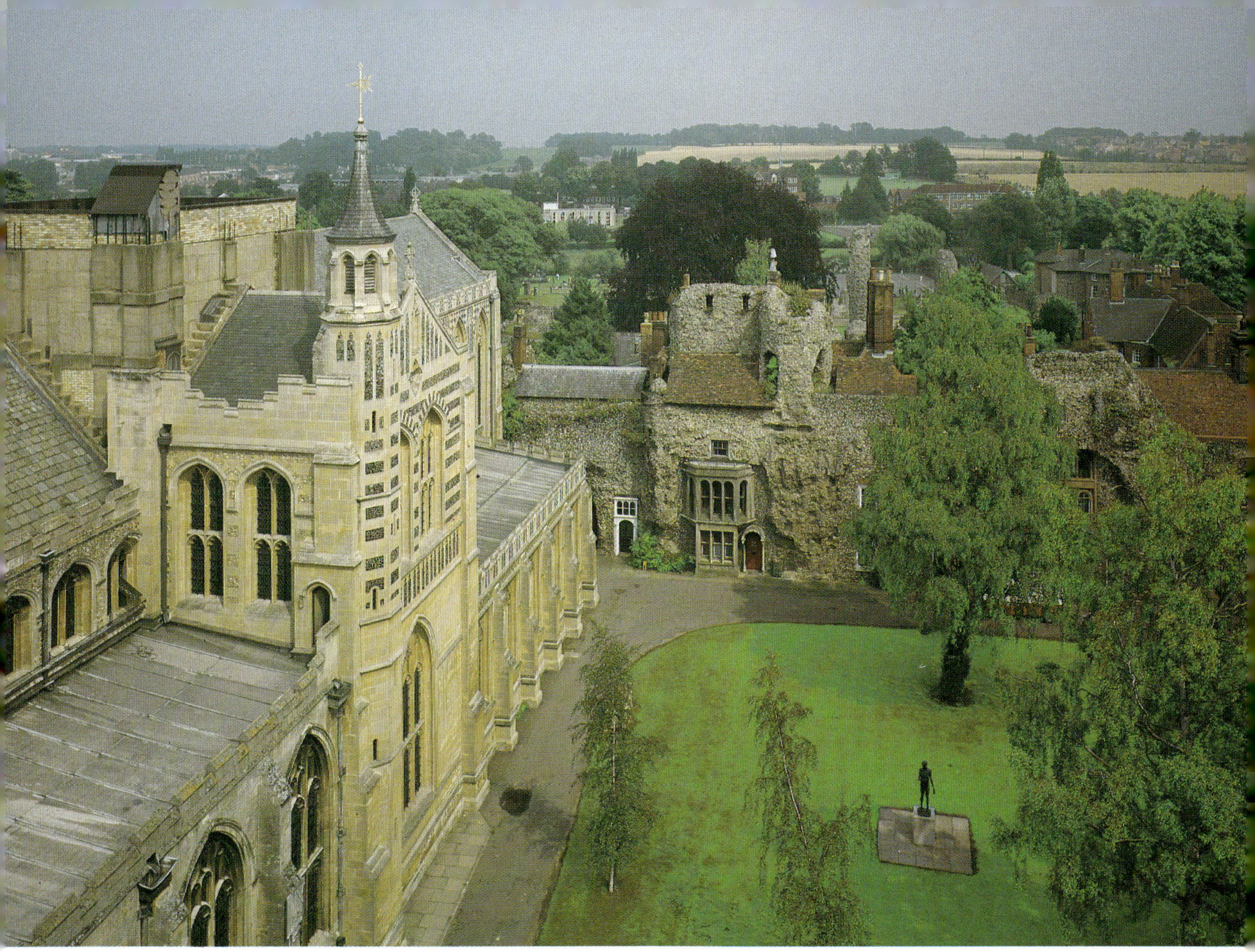

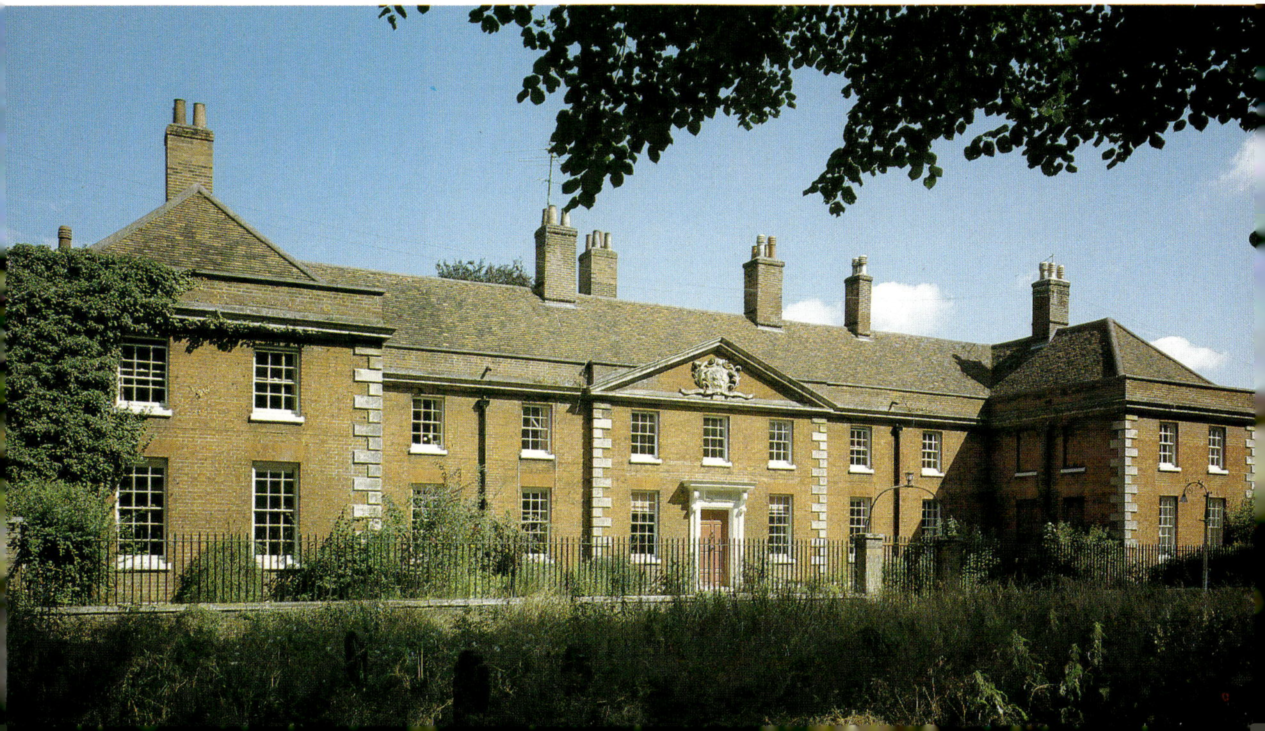

OFFA MEETS EDMVND IN SAXONY

✦ HAVERHILL SECONDARY SCHOOL ✦

IN COMMEMOR

PRESENTED, IN EDM

OF THE EAST-AN

EDMVND IS CROWNED KING

✦ BEYTON SECONDARY SCHOOL ✦

ATION OF THE

VND YEAR TO THE C

GLES : FOVNDER

BEODRICSWORTH BECOMES EDMVNDSTOWN

✦ SVDBVRY GIRLS HIGH SCHOOL ✦

1100th ANNIVE

ATHEDRAL AND ABBE

made the properties for the play, was asked to create a design for the tapestry which could be worked in panels independently by different schools, the whole to be subsequently joined into a long strip. The really beautiful properties he designed and made, in addition to a model in ivory coloured fibre glass of the beautiful Romanesque altar cross of carved walrus-ivory now in the possession of the Metropolitan Museum of Art in New York, were Bishop Humbert's cross and all the royal regalia and weapons. David Orchard was therefore a brilliant choice for the tapestry design.

Only the originator of the idea knew what creative love and industry the artist gave to the invention of his design. The Drama Centre in Bury St Edmunds was taken over for the whole of one weekend, the large hall darkened to aid concentration, and 40 feet of paper spread upon the floor to accommodate the placing of the design upon tracing paper. There, sustained by tea and sandwiches, the artist laboured and brought forth the design, acclaimed by all who see it.

When approached with the idea that secondary schools in the Liberty of St Edmundsbury should make the tapestry, the Chief Education Officer, Dr John Hill, gave every co-operation. All the secondary schools in the area were approached, and the following undertook to embroider a panel, under the general supervision of Miss Jane Page, of Dunmow, Essex, the regional representative of the Embroiderers' Guild:

Beyton Secondary School
Clare Secondary School
Convent of the Assumption, Hengrave
Girls' County Grammar School
Hadleigh Secondary School
Haverhill Secondary School
Ixworth Secondary School
Silver Jubilee Girls' School
Sudbury Girls' High School

Which town in England today can boast of its 'bayeux'?

When finished the panels were joined together so that the explanatory strip at top and bottom would be continuous, and the whole length (38′ × 9′ high) was presented to the cathedral authorities, who placed it on the unfinished wall of St Edmund's Chapel in the cathedral. After a moving ceremony of dedication the tapestry was handed over to the Provost, the Very Reverend John Waddington, M.B.E., T.D., M.A., by Dr John Hill on the 29th September 1970.

It was subsequently found that visitors constantly drawing an admiring hand over the work soiled the fabric. Eminent art authorities and glaziers were consulted. They advised against framing the whole length as it would be difficult to transport such a length of glass from the factory, and if it were broken, the cost of replacement would

be enormous. Therefore it was decided to frame each panel separately and Mrs Ironside Wood raised £498 to cover the cost.

The inscription along the top of the tapestry reads:

"EDMUND KING OF THE EAST ANGLES, FOUNDER OF BURY ST EDMUNDS, MARTYR FOR FAITH AND FREEDOM, MURDERED 870 ANNO DOMINI"

That along the bottom line reads:

"IN COMMEMORATION OF THE 1100th ANNIVERSARY OF THE MARTYRDOM OF ST EDMUND THIS TAPESTRY WAS MADE IN 1970"

The tapestry is illustrated as follows:

ABOVE: Panel 1 – Edmund meeting King Offa and his Queen at Hunstanton on his arrival from Saxony. – Haverhill Secondary School

Panel 2 – Edmund is crowned King of the Angles, seated in the Norman style. – Beyton Secondary School

Panel 3 – Beodricsworth becomes Edmundstown and the widow of the owner of the land offers a token of turf to Edmund. – Sudbury Girls' High School.

FACING PAGE ABOVE: Panel 4 – Lothparck, King of the Danes, was accidentally blown by fierce winds to the shores of East Anglia. Edmund treated him as an honoured guest until his jealous huntsman Berne murdered the King, when hunting in the forest. Berne is

FREEDOM: M

GOTHRUN BETRAYS EDMUND TO THE DANES

✦ HADLEIGH SECONDARY SCHOOL ✦

ND THIS TAP

SVFFOLK SCHOOLS

VRDERED 870

EDMUND IS CAPTURED & HUMBERT TORTURED

✦ CLARE SECONDARY SCHOOL ✦

ESTRY WAS M

DVRING EDMVND YE

ANNO DOMINI

THE MARTYRDOM OF EDMVND

✦ GIRLS' COVNTY GRAMMAR SCHOOL ✦

ADE IN 1970

AR

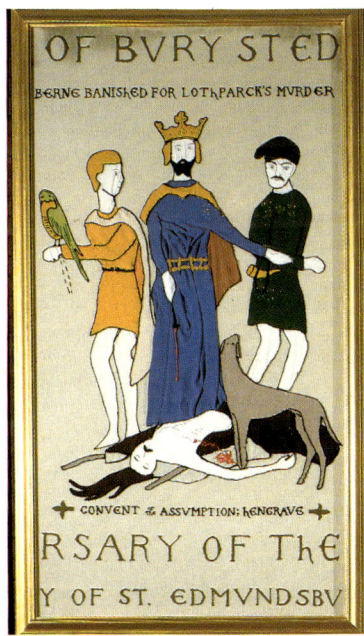

OF BVRY STED

BERNE BANISHED FOR LOTHPARCK'S MVRDER

✦ CONVENT of ASSVMPTION: HENGRAVE ✦

RSARY OF THE

Y OF ST. EDMVNDSBV

MVNDS: MARTYR

SACRARIVM · REGIS   CVNABVLA · LEGIS

✦ SILVER JVBILEE GIRLS SCHOOL ✦

MARTYRDOM

RY

FOR FAITH AND

INGVAR AND HVBBA SWEAR · MVRDER EDMVND

✦ IXWORTH SECONDARY SCHOOL ✦

OF ST. EDMV

WORKED IN WEST

banished. – Convent of the Assumption, Hengrave

Panel 5 – The arms of the old Borough of St Edmundsbury, incorporating the legend of the Martyr's head between the paws of a wolf, and the three crowns pierced by arrows – the motto is SACRARIUM REGIS CUNABULA REGIS (Shrine of a King, Cradle of the Law). – Silver Jubilee Girls' School

Panel 6 – Lothparck's sons, Inguar and Hubba, swear to murder Edmund in revenge. – Ixworth Secondary School

FACING PAGE BELOW: Panel 7 – Gothrum, a village girl, betrays Edmund to the Danes for gold. – Hadleigh Secondary School

Panel 8 – Edmund is captured. Bishop Humbert intervenes unsuccessfully and is tortured. – Clare Secondary School

Panel 9 – The martyrdom – Edmund is tied to an oak tree and asked to renounce Christ. He refuses, and the Danes kill him, cutting off his head, as was the pagan fashion, to prevent the victim haunting the killer. The head was thrown into the forest, where it was found by searching monks between the paws of a wolf. – Girls' County Grammar School

A Short History of the Kneelers

The idea behind the kneelers was to have a design in which there could be something in common throughout and yet would allow individual expression.

In the case of Suffolk it was felt that the spirit of unity in the diocese could best be illustrated by having a "Y" cross, an early symbol of Christianity, standing for the Church, while the diocese could conveniently and very adequately be represented by using the shades of blue by which in bygone days Suffolk cloth was known throughout Europe. To bring in the parishes each was accorded a motif, based either on the dedication of the parish or on some well known natural feature that links the mind with that particular parish. The worker could then express his or her self by the choice of stitches employed, and it is a feature of the kneelers that such a vast variation on a theme has been achieved. There are no two alike.

To get a thousand kneelers done might appear a daunting task till it is realised that there are just over five hundred parishes in the diocese, and therefore by calling on each parish for only two of this great number could be forthcoming.

In addition to the parishes there were other bodies who expressed interest and wished to join in, namely hospitals, schools, Guides, bell-ringers, and so on, and particular attention is drawn to the contributions of Free Churches.

The only way to deal with such a widely scattered community was to institute what really amounted to a postal course of instruction, for it must be borne in mind that for many workers this was their first venture into this type' of work.

As far as possible the work has been kept within the confines of the diocese and limited to those who can claim some close direct connection with Suffolk, though on occasion others have, by special plea, been included.

To all who have in any way contributed by money, work, or goodwill, we are immensely grateful.

★

ABOVE: *Some of the cathedral's 1,000 kneelers; there are no two alike.*

★

ACKNOWLEDGEMENTS
The text is based on the original Pitkin guide by the Very Rev John Waddington, M.B.E., T.D., M.A. with updates and amendments by the Very Rev Raymond Furnell (1985). All photographs were taken by Peter Smith, A.M.P.A of Newbery's, except the back cover which was taken by Aerofilms.

SBN 85372 104 1